Strictly for Cats

STRICTLY FOR CATS

First published as STRICTLY CAT DANCING in 2009
This edition copyright © Summersdale Publishers Ltd, 2015

Text by Anna Martin

All rights reserved.

Summersdale Publishers Ltd
46 West Street
Chichester
West Sussex
PO19 1RP
UK

www.summersdale.com

Printed and bound in China

ISBN: 978-1-84953-776-6

Substantial discounts on bulk quantities of Summersdale books are available to corporations, professional associations and other organisations. For details contact Nicky Douglas by telephone: +44 (0) 1243 756902, fax: +44 (0) 1243 786300 or email: nicky@summersdale.com.

Strictly for Cats

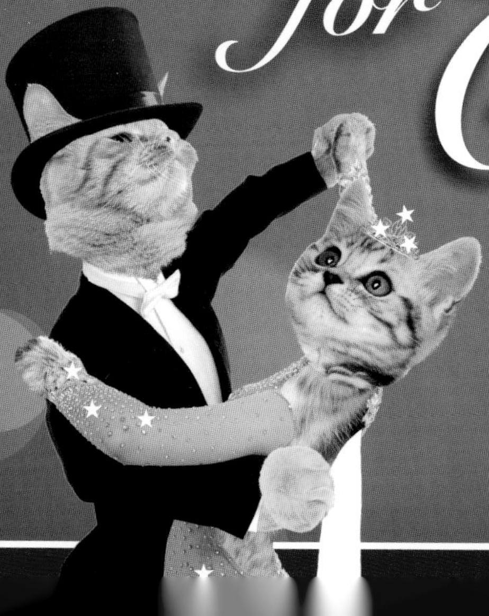

FELIX FOXTROT

Jasper: **"** *Time to shake your flea collars.* **"**

Bess: **"** *Welcome to Strictly for Cats!* **"**

Bess

Jasper

Fifi

Felix

Fifi: **"** Watch those lines, Felix! You look like you need a trip to the litter tray. **"**

Tommy: **"I'm just doing it for my mum… and the calendar contract."**

George

Mabel

Mabel: **"** *I didn't come on here to find love, but then I met George – meow!* **"**

Gaston: «'Ere's my 'andle and
'ere's my spout.»

Poppy: «I will scratch you if you
don't behave!»

Poppy

Gaston

Poppy: **"**I must prepare for lifting dead-weights if I'm to make it to the final.**"**

George: **"** *Oh, Mabel, I love a strong lady.* **"**

Fifi: **"***OMG, I've got a wedgie!***"**

Tommy: "Oh no, I have sweat
on my whiskers!
Quick, call my stylist."

Alberta

Tommy

Fifi

Felix

The Rumba –
Fifi and Felix

Felix: **"** *I can feel my talent
rising inside, or perhaps
it's a hairball...* **"**

Dolores: **"** *It's like watching a whale seduce a prawn.* **"**

4

Dolores

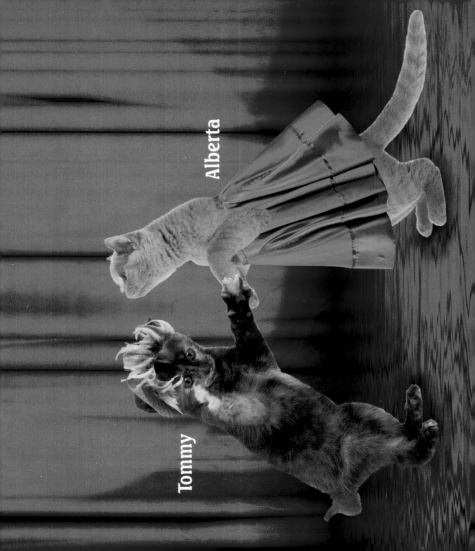

The Foxtrot –
Tommy and Alberta

Tommy: **"** Is this my best side? **"**

Alberta: **"** Concentrate, you nitwit! **"**

Ken: **"***Stiffer than a dead mouse, but not as tasty.***"**

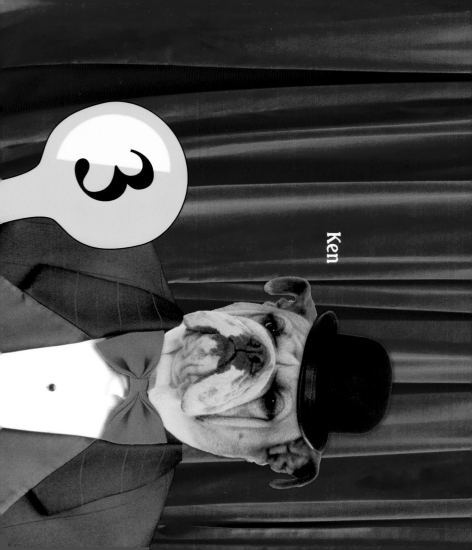

The Paso Doble –
George and Mabel

George: **❝** I'll be fine, as
long as I hold my
breath and smile! **❞**

Lorenzo: **"**Mabel looks like a glitter ball! It's time to lay off the kibble.**"**

Gaston

Poppy

The Jive –
Poppy and Gaston

Poppy: **"**Swing me by the
tail! I MUST win!**"**

Nigel: **"***All sauce, no steak!***"**

Nigel

Alberta

Tommy

The Samba –
Tommy and Alberta

Alberta: **❝** *You and your wool
fetish, Tommy. It's
like a cat's cradle.* **❞**

Dolores: **"**What an abomination! Like watching a spider devour its prey. **"**

Dolores

The Viennese Waltz –
George and Mabel

Mabel: **"** But you promised me
gold stars, not goldfish! **"**

Ken: **"** *I saw better moves when my cousin had a bad case of worms.* **"**

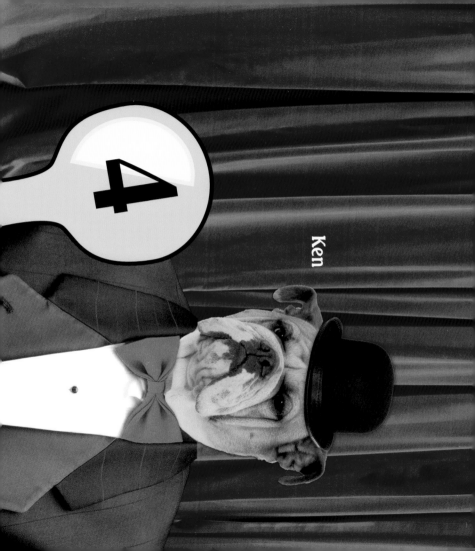

4

Ken

Gaston

Poppy

The Argentine Tango – Poppy and Gaston

Gaston: **"** *It's lucky I've been neutered – I would never have fitted into these pants otherwise.* **"**

Poppy: **"** *I see you brought lunch.* **"**

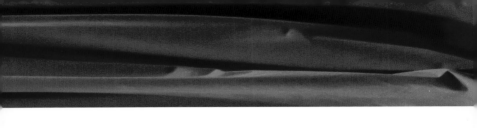

Lorenzo: **"** *The hamsters have more je ne sais quoi!* **"**

Mabel: **"** *It's MURDER on the dance floor!* **"**

George

Mabel

Poppy

Gaston

The Samba –
Poppy and Gaston

Poppy: **❝** *That's right; keep your focus away from my soft underbelly.* **❞**

Nigel: **❝***The flashiest piece of codswallop I've ever seen.***❞**

6

Nigel

Alberta

Tommy

The Rumba – Tommy and Alberta

Tommy: **"** *I can see my nine lives flashing in front of me!* **"**

Dolores: **"**I have never been so ashamed of the animal kingdom.**"**

2

Dolores

Bess: "If this display of feline frenzy doesn't get us an award, I'll eat my flea collar!"

Jasper: "A cat-astrophe!"

The judges prepare for the verdict...

Nigel

Lorenzo

Dolores: **"** *They're as bad as each other – it's Cat 22.* **"**

Ken

Dolores

Alberta: **"**I deserve to win – I can tap-dance and juggle mice simultaneously!**"**

Alberta

Tommy

Tommy: **"**_Only one of us can be top cat, and that is me!_**"**

Jasper: **"**You're all winners!
Keeeeeeep cat-dancing!**"**

Jasper

Well, that's it for another fab-u-lous season...

Gaston

Poppy

Fifi

Felix

... *let's head to the bar —*
I could really pounce on
a cocktail right now!

Tommy

Alberta

George

Mabel

Photo credits

Cat in tiara © Tad Denson • Cat with wide eyes © Condor 36 • Cat next to bottle © graphica • Large grey cat © Linn Currie • Large tabby cat © Tony Campbell • Ginger kitten © ZTS • Tortoiseshell kitten © Eric Isselée • Grey cat © Nelli Shuyskaya • Large ginger cat © Lars Christensen • Grey tabby kitten © Utekhina Anna • Black cat © Eric Isselée • White kitten © Tony Campbell • Red cat © Lee O'Dell • Bulldog © Eric Isselée • Naked cat © Suponev Vladimir Mihajlovich • Fat grey and white cat © Jasenka Lukša • Standing white kitten © Kirill Vorobyev • Stretching black cat -=PHANTOM=- • Grey tabby kitten © Yurchyks • Large ginger cat © Lars Christensen • Large tabby doing handstand © Efanov Aleksey Anatolievich • Ginger kitten yawning © Norman Chan • Large grey cat © Yurchyks • Ginger kitten © iofoto • Large tabby cat © Adi • Large grey cat © Perrush • Tortoiseshell kitten © Eric Isselée • Large ginger cat © Lars Christensen • Grey tabby kitten © Eric Isselée • Black cat © Eric Isselée • white kitten © enote • Cat with wide eyes © Condor 36 • Large grey cat © Tatiana Morozova • Grey cat ©ZTS • Ginger kitten © Dave Gordon • Large grey cat © Miramiska • Large white cat © graphica • white kitten © Tony Campbell • White kitten © Irving Lu • Tortoiseshell kitten © Lars Christensen • Grey tabby © Eric Isselée • Black cat © Eric Isselée • Large white cat © Irving Lu • Large grey cat © Tatiana Morozova • Tortoiseshell kitten © Eric Isselée • Grey cat © Agb • Grey tabby kitten © Eric

Isselée • Large ginger cat © Lars Christensen • Black cat © Eric Isselée • White kitten © Tony Campbell • Grey cats © Utekhina Anna • Shocked cat © Utekhina Anna • Sphinx kittens © Linn Currie • Ginger cat lying down © Gina Smith • Crying grey tabby © Eric Isselée • White kitten © Antonio Jorge Nunes • Tortoiseshell kitten © Eric Isselée • White kitten © Utekhina Anna • Bulldog © WillieCole • Large white cat © Irving Lu • Large grey cat © Linn Currie • Grey cat © Perrush • White kitten © Linn Currie • Red cat © Lee O'Dell • Ginger kitten © Eric Isselée • Tortoiseshell kitten © Eric Isselée • White cat © Tamila Aspen (TAStudio) • Red cat © Lee O'Dell • Bulldog © Eric Isselée • Naked cat © Suponev Vladimir Mihajlovich • Fat grey and white cat © Jasenka Lukša • Black cat © Eric Isselée • White kitten © Tony Campbell • Large grey cat © Tatiana Morozova • Large white cat © graphica • Grey cat stretching © Erik Lam • Tortoiseshell kitten stretching © Eric Isselée • Black kitten © Olga Mihajlovich • White kitten © Artem Kursin • Two white kittens © Linn Currie • Sphinx kitten © Linn Currie • Large white cat © Suzanne Tucker • Large grey cat © Tatiana Morozova • Red cat © Lee O'Dell • Bulldog © Eric Isselée • Naked cat © Suponev Vladimir Mihajlovich • Fat grey and white cat © Jasenka Lukša • Grey cat © Perrush • Large grey cat © Linn Currie • Laughing bulldog © WillieCole • White kitten © Antonio Jorge Nunes • Tortoiseshell kitten © Eric Isselée • Fat grey and white cat © Krissi Lundgren

CAT SELFIES

Charlie Ellis

ISBN: 978-1-84953-646-2

Hardback

£6.99

#glamourpusses

Everyone is snapping selfies and cats are no exception! From the sublime to the ridiculous, this book collects the best photos of felines who have taken the selfie craze into their own paws.

WHEN CATS TURN BAD

Kitty Litter

ISBN: 978-1-84024-784-8
Hardback
£5.99

They may look cute and fluffy, they may even appear affectionate – but don't be fooled. This is what happens when cats turn bad. It's not pretty.

These malicious moggies are rude, crude and foul-mouthed. Here at last is a book that exposes the cats' true agenda.

If you're interested in finding out more about our books, find us on Facebook at **Summersdale Publishers** and follow us on Twitter at **@Summersdale**.

www.summersdale.com